count *your* blessings

a 1-minute gratitude journal

a more faithful, happy you
in **1** minute a day

mia miller

count *your* blessings
a 1-minute gratitude journal

May the words
of my mouth
& the meditation
of my heart
be pleasing to you,
O LORD,
my rock &
my redeemer.

—Psalm 19:14

I'm grateful to you for buying & using this journal!

If you'd like to pay the gratitude forward, would you consider sharing it with others by leaving an Amazon review? It's the best way to help other people find this journal and bring more gratitude to their lives!

You can use this link to leave a review on Amazon:

http://bit.ly/blessingsjournal

or go to the page where you bought it and click "Leave a review."

THANK YOU!
Mia

introduction

I wrote this book because I needed it badly. Everything was going right in my life—I had a job I loved, a wonderful husband, a sweet daughter, a beautiful home, and enough food on the table. Yet I felt restless. Fussy. Like a newborn who wriggles and squirms and can't quite figure out why something feels off.

One day, I prayed to God, "Why am I always fussing? Why do I always zero in on what's wrong when everything overall is so right?"

I felt right then what I was missing: gratitude. I'd worked so hard to get to this wonderful point in my life, but now that I'd "arrived" I couldn't seem to lean back and enjoy it. I couldn't let go of striving so that I could settle into praising.

I vowed to make my intention for the year "praise, not planning." I wanted to see, *really see*, each little wonder that surrounded me, from my favorite white coffee mug in the morning, to the beautiful old tree swaying in the yard, to the way my daughter looks up at me as she's playing on the rug.

I wanted to open my eyes. And I needed God to do it for me.

I created this gratitude journal so that I could begin each day with what most matters: praising God + passing His love on to someone else.

Now, I spend just a minute or two each morning giving thanks to God for his glories in this gratitude journal. It helps me start my day in God's word, and I especially like that the Bible verses are from a variety of translations, as it gives fresh life to verses I've heard before. Of course, you could also end your day with this journal, and it would do just as much to renew your sense of joy and awe.

This one practice has completely changed my life. Instead of turning my first thought of the day to ticking off my to-do list, I turn it to counting the blessings God has given me and wants me to enjoy.

Just as importantly, I devote my first thoughts to ways I can spread God's love to others in small ways. These can be the simplest acts— sometimes it's nothing more than bringing donuts to the office on a dreary Tuesday or giving my daughter an extra 30 minutes of my full attention, even if it's just to talk about Paw Patrol again.

But I truly believe that these tiny acts of seeing people and helping them feel known and heard make a world of difference. I know that waking up to my own blessings has been life-changing, and I hope you, too, find that your days are brighter when you start or end them by counting your blessings.

Thank you so much for buying this gratitude journal and supporting me as a writer. If you enjoyed it, would you consider leaving a review on Amazon? It's the best way to help other people find this book, so we can all praise + pass it on a bit more! You can use this link if you'd like to leave a review: **http://bit.ly/blessingsjournal**.

Thank you so much, and wishing you all the blessings in the world,

Mia

"The materials were **sufficient** for them to do
all the work. There was **more than enough**."

— Exodus 36:7

today is: ....

3 blessings to count:

   1. ....

   2. ....

   3. ....

3 ways to bless others:

   1. ....

   2. ....

   3. ....

today is: ....

3 blessings to count:

   1. ....

   2. ....

   3. ....

3 ways to bless others:

   1. ....

   2. ....

   3. ....

today is: ....

3 blessings to count:

   1. ....

   2. ....

   3. ....

3 ways to bless others:

   1. ....

   2. ....

   3. ....

today is: ....

3 blessings to count:

   1. ....

   2. ....

   3. ....

3 ways to bless others:

   1. ....

   2. ....

   3. ....

"All this is for your benefit, so that the grace that is reaching more and more people may cause thanksgiving to overflow to the glory of God."

— 2 Corinthians 4:15

today is: ....

3 blessings to count:
1. ....
2. ....
3. ....

3 ways to bless others:
1. ....
2. ....
3. ....

today is: ....

3 blessings to count:
1. ....
2. ....
3. ....

3 ways to bless others:
1. ....
2. ....
3. ....

today is: ....

3 blessings to count:
1. ....
2. ....
3. ....

3 ways to bless others:
1. ....
2. ....
3. ....

today is: ....

3 blessings to count:
1. ....
2. ....
3. ....

3 ways to bless others:
1. ....
2. ....
3. ....

"I will give thanks to you, LORD, with **all my heart**;
I will tell of all **your wonderful deeds.**"

— Psalm 9:1

today is: ....

3 blessings to count:

   1. ....

   2. ....

   3. ....

3 ways to bless others:

   1. ....

   2. ....

   3. ....

today is: ....

3 blessings to count:

   1. ....

   2. ....

   3. ....

3 ways to bless others:

   1. ....

   2. ....

   3. ....

today is: ....

3 blessings to count:

   1. ....

   2. ....

   3. ....

3 ways to bless others:

   1. ....

   2. ....

   3. ....

today is: ....

3 blessings to count:

   1. ....

   2. ....

   3. ....

3 ways to bless others:

   1. ....

   2. ....

   3. ....

"Do not be anxious about anything, but in every situation, by prayer and petition, with thanksgiving, present your requests to God."
— Philippians 4:6

today is: ....

3 blessings to count:
   1. ....
   2. ....
   3. ....

3 ways to bless others:
   1. ....
   2. ....
   3. ....

today is: ....

3 blessings to count:
   1. ....
   2. ....
   3. ....

3 ways to bless others:
   1. ....
   2. ....
   3. ....

today is: ....

3 blessings to count:
   1. ....
   2. ....
   3. ....

3 ways to bless others:
   1. ....
   2. ....
   3. ....

today is: ....

3 blessings to count:
   1. ....
   2. ....
   3. ....

3 ways to bless others:
   1. ....
   2. ....
   3. ....

"Give **thanks** to the Lord, for he is **good**;
his love endures forever."

— 1 Chronicles 16:34

today is: ....

3 blessings to count:

   1. ....

   2. ....

   3. ....

3 ways to bless others:

   1. ....

   2. ....

   3. ....

---

today is: ....

3 blessings to count:

   1. ....

   2. ....

   3. ....

3 ways to bless others:

   1. ....

   2. ....

   3. ....

---

today is: ....

3 blessings to count:

   1. ....

   2. ....

   3. ....

3 ways to bless others:

   1. ....

   2. ....

   3. ....

---

today is: ....

3 blessings to count:

   1. ....

   2. ....

   3. ....

3 ways to bless others:

   1. ....

   2. ....

   3. ....

"Devote yourselves to prayer,
being *watchful* and *thankful."*

— Colossians 4:2

today is: ....

3 blessings to count:

1. ....
2. ....
3. ....

3 ways to bless others:

1. ....
2. ....
3. ....

today is: ....

3 blessings to count:

1. ....
2. ....
3. ....

3 ways to bless others:

1. ....
2. ....
3. ....

today is: ....

3 blessings to count:

1. ....
2. ....
3. ....

3 ways to bless others:

1. ....
2. ....
3. ....

today is: ....

3 blessings to count:

1. ....
2. ....
3. ....

3 ways to bless others:

1. ....
2. ....
3. ....

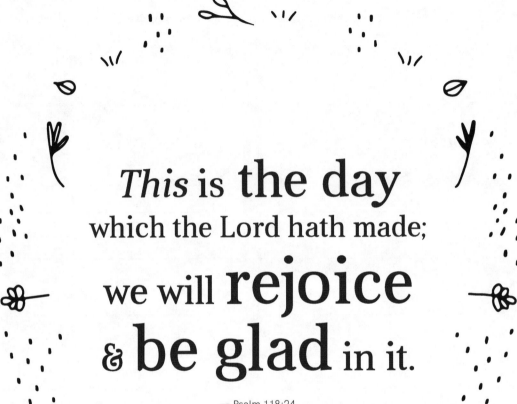

This is the day
which the Lord hath made;
we will **rejoice**
& **be glad** in it.

— Psalm 118:24

"Then I heard **every creature** in heaven and on earth and under the earth and on the sea, and all that is in them, saying: "To him who sits on the throne and to the Lamb be **praise and honor and glory and power**, for ever and ever!"

— Revelation 5:13

today is: ....

3 blessings to count:

1. ....
2. ....
3. ....

3 ways to bless others:

1. ....
2. ....
3. ....

today is: ....

3 blessings to count:

1. ....
2. ....
3. ....

3 ways to bless others:

1. ....
2. ....
3. ....

today is: ....

3 blessings to count:

1. ....
2. ....
3. ....

3 ways to bless others:

1. ....
2. ....
3. ....

today is: ....

3 blessings to count:

1. ....
2. ....
3. ....

3 ways to bless others:

1. ....
2. ....
3. ....

"But I, with shouts of grateful praise, will sacrifice to you.
What I have vowed I will make good.
I will say, 'Salvation comes from the Lord.'"

— Jonah 2:9

today is:........................

3 blessings to count:

1. ....

2. ....

3. ....

3 ways to bless others:

1. ....

2. ....

3. ....

today is:........................

3 blessings to count:

1. ....

2. ....

3. ....

3 ways to bless others:

1. ....

2. ....

3. ....

today is:........................

3 blessings to count:

1. ....

2. ....

3. ....

3 ways to bless others:

1. ....

2. ....

3. ....

today is:........................

3 blessings to count:

1. ....

2. ....

3. ....

3 ways to bless others:

1. ....

2. ....

3. ....

"But thanks be to God!
He gives us the victory through our Lord Jesus Christ."
— 1 Corinthians 15:57

🌸 today is: ....

3 blessings to count:

1. ....

2. ....

3. ....

3 ways to bless others:

1. ....

2. ....

3. ....

⬭ today is: ....

3 blessings to count:

1. ....

2. ....

3. ....

3 ways to bless others:

1. ....

2. ....

3. ....

---

today is: ....

3 blessings to count:

1. ....

2. ....

3. ....

3 ways to bless others:

1. ....

2. ....

3. ....

---

today is: ....

3 blessings to count:

1. ....

2. ....

3. ....

3 ways to bless others:

1. ....

2. ....

3. ....

"Let your roots grow down into him, and let your lives be built on him.
Then your faith will grow strong in the truth you were taught,
and you will overflow with thankfulness."

— Psalm 9:1

today is:..................

3 blessings to count:

1. ....
2. ....
3. ....

3 ways to bless others:

1. ....
2. ....
3. ....

today is:..................

3 blessings to count:

1. ....
2. ....
3. ....

3 ways to bless others:

1. ....
2. ....
3. ....

today is:..................

3 blessings to count:

1. ....
2. ....
3. ....

3 ways to bless others:

1. ....
2. ....
3. ....

today is:..................

3 blessings to count:

1. ....
2. ....
3. ....

3 ways to bless others:

1. ....
2. ....
3. ....

"Giving thanks **always for all things** unto God and the Father
in the name of our Lord Jesus Christ."
— Ephesians 5:20

today is: ....

3 blessings to count:

1. ....
2. ....
3. ....

3 ways to bless others:

1. ....
2. ....
3. ....

today is: ....

3 blessings to count:

1. ....
2. ....
3. ....

3 ways to bless others:

1. ....
2. ....
3. ....

today is: ....

3 blessings to count:

1. ....
2. ....
3. ....

3 ways to bless others:

1. ....
2. ....
3. ....

today is: ....

3 blessings to count:

1. ....
2. ....
3. ....

3 ways to bless others:

1. ....
2. ....
3. ....

"This is the day which the Lord hath made;
we will rejoice and be glad in it."
— Psalm 118:24

---

today is: ....

3 blessings to count:

   1. ....

   2. ....

   3. ....

3 ways to bless others:

   1. ....

   2. ....

   3. ....

---

today is: ....

3 blessings to count:

   1. ....

   2. ....

   3. ....

3 ways to bless others:

   1. ....

   2. ....

   3. ....

---

today is: ....

3 blessings to count:

   1. ....

   2. ....

   3. ....

3 ways to bless others:

   1. ....

   2. ....

   3. ....

---

today is: ....

3 blessings to count:

   1. ....

   2. ....

   3. ....

3 ways to bless others:

   1. ....

   2. ....

   3. ....

"The one who offers thanksgiving as his sacrifice glorifies me;
to one who orders his way rightly I will show the salvation of God!"
— Psalm 50:23

today is: ....

3 blessings to count:

1. ....
2. ....
3. ....

3 ways to bless others:

1. ....
2. ....
3. ....

today is: ....

3 blessings to count:

1. ....
2. ....
3. ....

3 ways to bless others:

1. ....
2. ....
3. ....

today is: ....

3 blessings to count:

1. ....
2. ....
3. ....

3 ways to bless others:

1. ....
2. ....
3. ....

today is: ....

3 blessings to count:

1. ....
2. ....
3. ....

3 ways to bless others:

1. ....
2. ....
3. ....

"The Lord is my strength and my shield; my heart trusts in him, and he helps me. My heart leaps for joy, and with my song I praise him."

— Psalm 28:7

---

today is: ....

3 blessings to count:

1. ....
2. ....
3. ....

3 ways to bless others:

1. ....
2. ....
3. ....

---

today is: ....

3 blessings to count:

1. ....
2. ....
3. ....

3 ways to bless others:

1. ....
2. ....
3. ....

---

today is: ....

3 blessings to count:

1. ....
2. ....
3. ....

3 ways to bless others:

1. ....
2. ....
3. ....

---

today is: ....

3 blessings to count:

1. ....
2. ....
3. ....

3 ways to bless others:

1. ....
2. ....
3. ....

Mercy,
peace,
& love
be yours in
abundance.

— Jude 1:2

"May the God of hope **fill you with all joy** and peace as you trust in him, so that you may **overflow with hope** by the power of the Holy Spirit."

— Romans 15:13

today is: ....

3 blessings to count:

   1. ....

   2. ....

   3. ....

3 ways to bless others:

   1. ....

   2. ....

   3. ....

today is: ....

3 blessings to count:

   1. ....

   2. ....

   3. ....

3 ways to bless others:

   1. ....

   2. ....

   3. ....

today is: ....

3 blessings to count:

   1. ....

   2. ....

   3. ....

3 ways to bless others:

   1. ....

   2. ....

   3. ....

today is: ....

3 blessings to count:

   1. ....

   2. ....

   3. ....

3 ways to bless others:

   1. ....

   2. ....

   3. ....

"They are to do good, to be rich in good works,
to be generous & ready to share,
thus storing up treasure for themselves as a good foundation for the future."

— 1 Timothy 6:18

today is: ....

3 blessings to count:

1. ....
2. ....
3. ....

3 ways to bless others:

1. ....
2. ....
3. ....

today is: ....

3 blessings to count:

1. ....
2. ....
3. ....

3 ways to bless others:

1. ....
2. ....
3. ....

today is: ....

3 blessings to count:

1. ....
2. ....
3. ....

3 ways to bless others:

1. ....
2. ....
3. ....

today is: ....

3 blessings to count:

1. ....
2. ....
3. ....

3 ways to bless others:

1. ....
2. ....
3. ....

"Devote yourselves to prayer, being watchful & thankful."

— Colossians 4:2

today is: ....

3 blessings to count:

1. ....

2. ....

3. ....

3 ways to bless others:

1. ....

2. ....

3. ....

today is: ....

3 blessings to count:

1. ....

2. ....

3. ....

3 ways to bless others:

1. ....

2. ....

3. ....

today is: ....

3 blessings to count:

1. ....

2. ....

3. ....

3 ways to bless others:

1. ....

2. ....

3. ....

today is: ....

3 blessings to count:

1. ....

2. ....

3. ....

3 ways to bless others:

1. ....

2. ....

3. ....

"So we fix our eyes not on what is seen, but on what is unseen, since what is seen is temporary, but **what is unseen is eternal.**"

— 2 Corinthians 4:18

today is: ....

3 blessings to count:

  1. ....
  2. ....
  3. ....

3 ways to bless others:

  1. ....
  2. ....
  3. ....

today is: ....

3 blessings to count:

  1. ....
  2. ....
  3. ....

3 ways to bless others:

  1. ....
  2. ....
  3. ....

today is: ....

3 blessings to count:

  1. ....
  2. ....
  3. ....

3 ways to bless others:

  1. ....
  2. ....
  3. ....

today is: ....

3 blessings to count:

  1. ....
  2. ....
  3. ....

3 ways to bless others:

  1. ....
  2. ....
  3. ....

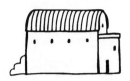

"May God give you **heaven's dew and earth's richness**
—an abundance of grain and new wine."
— Genesis 27:28

today is: ....

3 blessings to count:
   1. ....
   2. ....
   3. ....

3 ways to bless others:
   1. ....
   2. ....
   3. ....

today is: ....

3 blessings to count:
   1. ....
   2. ....
   3. ....

3 ways to bless others:
   1. ....
   2. ....
   3. ....

today is: ....

3 blessings to count:
   1. ....
   2. ....
   3. ....

3 ways to bless others:
   1. ....
   2. ....
   3. ....

today is: ....

3 blessings to count:
   1. ....
   2. ....
   3. ....

3 ways to bless others:
   1. ....
   2. ....
   3. ....

"Commit to the Lord whatever you do,
& he will establish your plans."

— Proverbs 16:3

---

today is: ....

3 blessings to count:

1. ....
2. ....
3. ....

3 ways to bless others:

1. ....
2. ....
3. ....

---

today is: ....

3 blessings to count:

1. ....
2. ....
3. ....

3 ways to bless others:

1. ....
2. ....
3. ....

---

today is: ....

3 blessings to count:

1. ....
2. ....
3. ....

3 ways to bless others:

1. ....
2. ....
3. ....

---

today is: ....

3 blessings to count:

1. ....
2. ....
3. ....

3 ways to bless others:

1. ....
2. ....
3. ....

"If you follow my decrees and are careful to obey my commands,
I will send you rain in its season,
and the ground will yield its crops & the trees their fruit."
— Leviticus 26:3-4

today is: ....

3 blessings to count:

   1. ....

   2. ....

   3. ....

3 ways to bless others:

   1. ....

   2. ....

   3. ....

today is: ....

3 blessings to count:

   1. ....

   2. ....

   3. ....

3 ways to bless others:

   1. ....

   2. ....

   3. ....

today is: ....

3 blessings to count:

   1. ....

   2. ....

   3. ....

3 ways to bless others:

   1. ....

   2. ....

   3. ....

today is: ....

3 blessings to count:

   1. ....

   2. ....

   3. ....

3 ways to bless others:

   1. ....

   2. ....

   3. ....

"Sing and make music from your heart to the Lord,
always giving thanks to God the Father for everything,
in the name of our Lord Jesus Christ."

— Ephesians 5:19-20

today is: ....

3 blessings to count:

1. ....

2. ....

3. ....

3 ways to bless others:

1. ....

2. ....

3. ....

today is: ....

3 blessings to count:

1. ....

2. ....

3. ....

3 ways to bless others:

1. ....

2. ....

3. ....

today is: ....

3 blessings to count:

1. ....

2. ....

3. ....

3 ways to bless others:

1. ....

2. ....

3. ....

today is: ....

3 blessings to count:

1. ....

2. ....

3. ....

3 ways to bless others:

1. ....

2. ....

3. ....

"Cast all your anxiety on Him
because he cares for you."

— 1 Peter 5:7

---

today is: ....

3 blessings to count:

   1. ....

   2. ....

   3. ....

3 ways to bless others:

   1. ....

   2. ....

   3. ....

---

today is: ....

3 blessings to count:

   1. ....

   2. ....

   3. ....

3 ways to bless others:

   1. ....

   2. ....

   3. ....

---

today is: ....

3 blessings to count:

   1. ....

   2. ....

   3. ....

3 ways to bless others:

   1. ....

   2. ....

   3. ....

---

today is: ....

3 blessings to count:

   1. ....

   2. ....

   3. ....

3 ways to bless others:

   1. ....

   2. ....

   3. ....

Let your roots grow down into him,
and let your lives be built on him.
Then your faith will grow strong
in the truth you were taught,
and you will overflow
with thankfulness.

— Psalm 9:1

"For everything God created is good,
and nothing is to be rejected if it is received with thanksgiving,
because it is consecrated by the word of God and prayer."

— 1 Timothy 4:4-5

today is: ....

3 blessings to count:

1. ....
2. ....
3. ....

3 ways to bless others:

1. ....
2. ....
3. ....

today is: ....

3 blessings to count:

1. ....
2. ....
3. ....

3 ways to bless others:

1. ....
2. ....
3. ....

today is: ....

3 blessings to count:

1. ....
2. ....
3. ....

3 ways to bless others:

1. ....
2. ....
3. ....

today is: ....

3 blessings to count:

1. ....
2. ....
3. ....

3 ways to bless others:

1. ....
2. ....
3. ....

"And whatever you do, **whether in word or deed,**
do it all in the name of the Lord Jesus,
giving thanks to God the Father through him."
— Colossians 3:17

today is: ....

3 blessings to count:

1. ....
2. ....
3. ....

3 ways to bless others:

1. ....
2. ....
3. ....

today is: ....

3 blessings to count:

1. ....
2. ....
3. ....

3 ways to bless others:

1. ....
2. ....
3. ....

today is: ....

3 blessings to count:

1. ....
2. ....
3. ....

3 ways to bless others:

1. ....
2. ....
3. ....

today is: ....

3 blessings to count:

1. ....
2. ....
3. ....

3 ways to bless others:

1. ....
2. ....
3. ....

"Now to him who is able to do **immeasurably** more than all we ask or imagine, according to his power that is at work within us."

— Ephesians 3:20

today is: ....

3 blessings to count:

1. ....

2. ....

3. ....

3 ways to bless others:

1. ....

2. ....

3. ....

today is: ....

3 blessings to count:

1. ....

2. ....

3. ....

3 ways to bless others:

1. ....

2. ....

3. ....

today is: ....

3 blessings to count:

1. ....

2. ....

3. ....

3 ways to bless others:

1. ....

2. ....

3. ....

today is: ....

3 blessings to count:

1. ....

2. ....

3. ....

3 ways to bless others:

1. ....

2. ....

3. ....

"Enter into his gates with thanksgiving, and into his courts with praise: be thankful unto him, and bless his name."

— Psalm 100:4

today is: _____

3 blessings to count:
1. _____
2. _____
3. _____

3 ways to bless others:
1. _____
2. _____
3. _____

today is: _____

3 blessings to count:
1. _____
2. _____
3. _____

3 ways to bless others:
1. _____
2. _____
3. _____

today is: _____

3 blessings to count:
1. _____
2. _____
3. _____

3 ways to bless others:
1. _____
2. _____
3. _____

today is: _____

3 blessings to count:
1. _____
2. _____
3. _____

3 ways to bless others:
1. _____
2. _____
3. _____

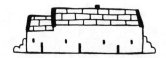

"You will be enriched in every way so that you can
be generous on every occasion,
and through us your generosity will result in thanksgiving to God."

— 2 Corinthians 9:11

today is: ....

3 blessings to count:

   1. ....

   2. ....

   3. ....

3 ways to bless others:

   1. ....

   2. ....

   3. ....

today is: ....

3 blessings to count:

   1. ....

   2. ....

   3. ....

3 ways to bless others:

   1. ....

   2. ....

   3. ....

today is: ....

3 blessings to count:

   1. ....

   2. ....

   3. ....

3 ways to bless others:

   1. ....

   2. ....

   3. ....

today is: ....

3 blessings to count:

   1. ....

   2. ....

   3. ....

3 ways to bless others:

   1. ....

   2. ....

   3. ....

"Let them give thanks to the Lord for his unfailing love
and his wonderful deeds for mankind,
for he satisfies the thirsty and fills the hungry with good things."
— Psalm 107:8-9

today is: ....

3 blessings to count:

1. ....

2. ....

3. ....

3 ways to bless others:

1. ....

2. ....

3. ....

today is: ....

3 blessings to count:

1. ....

2. ....

3. ....

3 ways to bless others:

1. ....

2. ....

3. ....

today is: ....

3 blessings to count:

1. ....

2. ....

3. ....

3 ways to bless others:

1. ....

2. ....

3. ....

today is: ....

3 blessings to count:

1. ....

2. ....

3. ....

3 ways to bless others:

1. ....

2. ....

3. ....

"And my God will meet all your needs
according to the riches of his glory in Christ Jesus." "
— Philippians 4:19

🍍 today is: ....

3 blessings to count:

1. ....
2. ....
3. ....

3 ways to bless others:

1. ....
2. ....
3. ....

🌿 today is: ....

3 blessings to count:

1. ....
2. ....
3. ....

3 ways to bless others:

1. ....
2. ....
3. ....

🌺 today is: ....

3 blessings to count:

1. ....
2. ....
3. ....

3 ways to bless others:

1. ....
2. ....
3. ....

🌷 today is: ....

3 blessings to count:

1. ....
2. ....
3. ....

3 ways to bless others:

1. ....
2. ....
3. ....

"Trust in the Lord with all your heart and lean not on your own understanding."

— Proverbs 3:5

today is: ....

3 blessings to count:

1. ....

2. ....

3. ....

3 ways to bless others:

1. ....

2. ....

3. ....

today is: ....

3 blessings to count:

1. ....

2. ....

3. ....

3 ways to bless others:

1. ....

2. ....

3. ....

today is: ....

3 blessings to count:

1. ....

2. ....

3. ....

3 ways to bless others:

1. ....

2. ....

3. ....

today is: ....

3 blessings to count:

1. ....

2. ....

3. ....

3 ways to bless others:

1. ....

2. ....

3. ....

"May the Lord, the God of your fathers, increase you a thousand-fold more than you are and bless you, just as He has promised you!"
— Deutoronomy 1:11

today is: ....

3 blessings to count:

   1. ....

   2. ....

   3. ....

3 ways to bless others:

   1. ....

   2. ....

   3. ....

today is: ....

3 blessings to count:

   1. ....

   2. ....

   3. ....

3 ways to bless others:

   1. ....

   2. ....

   3. ....

today is: ....

3 blessings to count:

   1. ....

   2. ....

   3. ....

3 ways to bless others:

   1. ....

   2. ....

   3. ....

today is: ....

3 blessings to count:

   1. ....

   2. ....

   3. ....

3 ways to bless others:

   1. ....

   2. ....

   3. ....

"You will make known to me the path of life;
in Your presence is fullness of joy;
in Your right hand there are pleasures forever."

— Psalm 16:11

today is: ....

3 blessings to count:

1. ....

2. ....

3. ....

3 ways to bless others:

1. ....

2. ....

3. ....

today is: ....

3 blessings to count:

1. ....

2. ....

3. ....

3 ways to bless others:

1. ....

2. ....

3. ....

today is: ....

3 blessings to count:

1. ....

2. ....

3. ....

3 ways to bless others:

1. ....

2. ....

3. ....

today is: ....

3 blessings to count:

1. ....

2. ....

3. ....

3 ways to bless others:

1. ....

2. ....

3. ....

Trust in the Lord with
all your heart
and lean not
on your own understanding.
--proverbs 3:5

Listen, my son,
accept what I say, and
the years of your life
will be many.

--proverbs 4:10

Commit

to the Lord whatever you do,
and he will establish your plans.

--proverbs 16:3

"And you will know the truth,
and the truth will set you free."
— John 8:32

---

today is: ....

3 blessings to count:

  1. ....
  2. ....
  3. ....

3 ways to bless others:

  1. ....
  2. ....
  3. ....

---

today is: ....

3 blessings to count:

  1. ....
  2. ....
  3. ....

3 ways to bless others:

  1. ....
  2. ....
  3. ....

---

today is: ....

3 blessings to count:

  1. ....
  2. ....
  3. ....

3 ways to bless others:

  1. ....
  2. ....
  3. ....

---

today is: ....

3 blessings to count:

  1. ....
  2. ....
  3. ....

3 ways to bless others:

  1. ....
  2. ....
  3. ....

"Be transformed by the renewal of your mind,
that by testing you may discern what is **the will of God**,
what is **good & acceptable & perfect.**"

— Romans 12:2

today is: ....

3 blessings to count:

1. ....
2. ....
3. ....

3 ways to bless others:

1. ....
2. ....
3. ....

today is: ....

3 blessings to count:

1. ....
2. ....
3. ....

3 ways to bless others:

1. ....
2. ....
3. ....

today is: ....

3 blessings to count:

1. ....
2. ....
3. ....

3 ways to bless others:

1. ....
2. ....
3. ....

today is: ....

3 blessings to count:

1. ....
2. ....
3. ....

3 ways to bless others:

1. ....
2. ....
3. ....

"I will give you thanks in the great assembly;
among the throngs **I will praise you.**"
— Psalm 35:18

today is: ....

3 blessings to count:
   1. ....
   2. ....
   3. ....

3 ways to bless others:
   1. ....
   2. ....
   3. ....

today is: ....

3 blessings to count:
   1. ....
   2. ....
   3. ....

3 ways to bless others:
   1. ....
   2. ....
   3. ....

today is: ....

3 blessings to count:
   1. ....
   2. ....
   3. ....

3 ways to bless others:
   1. ....
   2. ....
   3. ....

today is: ....

3 blessings to count:
   1. ....
   2. ....
   3. ....

3 ways to bless others:
   1. ....
   2. ....
   3. ....

"Then we your people, the sheep of your pasture, will praise you forever; from generation to generation **we will proclaim your praise**."

— Psalm 79:13

⟿⟾⟾⟵ today is: ....

3 blessings to count:

1. ....

2. ....

3. ....

3 ways to bless others:

1. ....

2. ....

3. ....

🏷 today is: ....

3 blessings to count:

1. ....

2. ....

3. ....

3 ways to bless others:

1. ....

2. ....

3. ....

🌿 today is: ....

3 blessings to count:

1. ....

2. ....

3. ....

3 ways to bless others:

1. ....

2. ....

3. ....

🌱 today is: ....

3 blessings to count:

1. ....

2. ....

3. ....

3 ways to bless others:

1. ....

2. ....

3. ....

"For the LORD is good and his love endures forever;
his faithfulness continues through all generations."
— Psalm 100:5

today is: ....

3 blessings to count:

1. ....

2. ....

3. ....

3 ways to bless others:

1. ....

2. ....

3. ....

today is: ....

3 blessings to count:

1. ....

2. ....

3. ....

3 ways to bless others:

1. ....

2. ....

3. ....

today is: ....

3 blessings to count:

1. ....

2. ....

3. ....

3 ways to bless others:

1. ....

2. ....

3. ....

today is: ....

3 blessings to count:

1. ....

2. ....

3. ....

3 ways to bless others:

1. ....

2. ....

3. ....

"And the peace of God, which **transcends all understanding,**
will guard your hearts and your minds in Christ Jesus."

— Philippians 4:7

---

today is: ....

3 blessings to count:

1. ....

2. ....

3. ....

3 ways to bless others:

1. ....

2. ....

3. ....

---

today is: ....

3 blessings to count:

1. ....

2. ....

3. ....

3 ways to bless others:

1. ....

2. ....

3. ....

---

today is: ....

3 blessings to count:

1. ....

2. ....

3. ....

3 ways to bless others:

1. ....

2. ....

3. ....

---

today is: ....

3 blessings to count:

1. ....

2. ....

3. ....

3 ways to bless others:

1. ....

2. ....

3. ....

"Praise the Lord, my soul; all my inmost being, praise his holy name.
Praise the Lord, my soul, and forget not all his benefits."
— Psalm 103:1-3

today is: ....

3 blessings to count:

   1. ....

   2. ....

   3. ....

3 ways to bless others:

   1. ....

   2. ....

   3. ....

today is: ....

3 blessings to count:

   1. ....

   2. ....

   3. ....

3 ways to bless others:

   1. ....

   2. ....

   3. ....

today is: ....

3 blessings to count:

   1. ....

   2. ....

   3. ....

3 ways to bless others:

   1. ....

   2. ....

   3. ....

today is: ....

3 blessings to count:

   1. ....

   2. ....

   3. ....

3 ways to bless others:

   1. ....

   2. ....

   3. ....

"Therefore, since we are receiving a kingdom that cannot be shaken,
let us be thankful, and so worship God acceptably with
reverence and awe."

— Hebrews 12:28

today is: _____

3 blessings to count:

1. ....

2. ....

3. ....

3 ways to bless others:

1. ....

2. ....

3. ....

today is: _____

3 blessings to count:

1. ....

2. ....

3. ....

3 ways to bless others:

1. ....

2. ....

3. ....

today is: _____

3 blessings to count:

1. ....

2. ....

3. ....

3 ways to bless others:

1. ....

2. ....

3. ....

today is: _____

3 blessings to count:

1. ....

2. ....

3. ....

3 ways to bless others:

1. ....

2. ....

3. ....

"Save us, Lord our God, and gather us from the nations,
that we may give thanks to your holy name and glory in your praise."

— Psalm 106:47

today is: ....

3 blessings to count:

1. ....

2. ....

3. ....

3 ways to bless others:

1. ....

2. ....

3. ....

today is: ....

3 blessings to count:

1. ....

2. ....

3. ....

3 ways to bless others:

1. ....

2. ....

3. ....

today is: ....

3 blessings to count:

1. ....

2. ....

3. ....

3 ways to bless others:

1. ....

2. ....

3. ....

today is: ....

3 blessings to count:

1. ....

2. ....

3. ....

3 ways to bless others:

1. ....

2. ....

3. ....

"The Lord gives **strength** to his people;
the Lord blesses his people with **peace**."

— Psalm 29:11

today is: ....

3 blessings to count:

1. ....

2. ....

3. ....

3 ways to bless others:

1. ....

2. ....

3. ....

today is: ....

3 blessings to count:

1. ....

2. ....

3. ....

3 ways to bless others:

1. ....

2. ....

3. ....

today is: ....

3 blessings to count:

1. ....

2. ....

3. ....

3 ways to bless others:

1. ....

2. ....

3. ....

today is: ....

3 blessings to count:

1. ....

2. ....

3. ....

3 ways to bless others:

1. ....

2. ....

3. ....

In
every
thing
give thanks.

— 1 Thessalonians 5:18

"But the **fruit of the Spirit** is love, joy, peace, forbearance, kindness, goodness, faithfulness, gentleness, and self-control."
— Galatians 5:22

---

today is: ....

3 blessings to count:

   1. ....
   2. ....
   3. ....

3 ways to bless others:

   1. ....
   2. ....
   3. ....

---

today is: ....

3 blessings to count:

   1. ....
   2. ....
   3. ....

3 ways to bless others:

   1. ....
   2. ....
   3. ....

---

today is: ....

3 blessings to count:

   1. ....
   2. ....
   3. ....

3 ways to bless others:

   1. ....
   2. ....
   3. ....

---

today is: ....

3 blessings to count:

   1. ....
   2. ....
   3. ....

3 ways to bless others:

   1. ....
   2. ....
   3. ....

"From the Lord comes deliverance.
May your blessing be on your people."

— Psalm 3:8

---

today is: ....

3 blessings to count:

1. ....
2. ....
3. ....

3 ways to bless others:

1. ....
2. ....
3. ....

---

today is: ....

3 blessings to count:

1. ....
2. ....
3. ....

3 ways to bless others:

1. ....
2. ....
3. ....

---

today is: ....

3 blessings to count:

1. ....
2. ....
3. ....

3 ways to bless others:

1. ....
2. ....
3. ....

---

today is: ....

3 blessings to count:

1. ....
2. ....
3. ....

3 ways to bless others:

1. ....
2. ....
3. ....

"The **blessing of the Lord** brings wealth,
without painful toil for it."

— Proverbs 10:22

today is: ....

3 blessings to count:

1. ....

2. ....

3. ....

3 ways to bless others:

1. ....

2. ....

3. ....

today is: ....

3 blessings to count:

1. ....

2. ....

3. ....

3 ways to bless others:

1. ....

2. ....

3. ....

today is: ....

3 blessings to count:

1. ....

2. ....

3. ....

3 ways to bless others:

1. ....

2. ....

3. ....

today is: ....

3 blessings to count:

1. ....

2. ....

3. ....

3 ways to bless others:

1. ....

2. ....

3. ....

"How abundant are the good things that you have stored up for those who **fear you**, that you bestow in the sight of all, on those who **take refuge in you**."

— Psalm 31:19

today is: ....

3 blessings to count:

1. ....
2. ....
3. ....

3 ways to bless others:

1. ....
2. ....
3. ....

today is: ....

3 blessings to count:

1. ....
2. ....
3. ....

3 ways to bless others:

1. ....
2. ....
3. ....

today is: ....

3 blessings to count:

1. ....
2. ....
3. ....

3 ways to bless others:

1. ....
2. ....
3. ....

today is: ....

3 blessings to count:

1. ....
2. ....
3. ....

3 ways to bless others:

1. ....
2. ....
3. ....

For the Lord takes delight in his people;
he crowns the humble with victory."
— Psalm 149:4

🌿 today is: ....

3 blessings to count:
  1. ....
  2. ....
  3. ....

3 ways to bless others:
  1. ....
  2. ....
  3. ....

🍍 today is: ....

3 blessings to count:
  1. ....
  2. ....
  3. ....

3 ways to bless others:
  1. ....
  2. ....
  3. ....

✎ today is: ....

3 blessings to count:
  1. ....
  2. ....
  3. ....

3 ways to bless others:
  1. ....
  2. ....
  3. ....

📷 today is: ....

3 blessings to count:
  1. ....
  2. ....
  3. ....

3 ways to bless others:
  1. ....
  2. ....
  3. ....

"The Lord bless you and keep you;
the Lord make his face shine on you and be gracious to you;
the Lord turn his face toward you and give you peace."

— Numbers 6:24-26

today is: ....

3 blessings to count:

1. ....

2. ....

3. ....

3 ways to bless others:

1. ....

2. ....

3. ....

today is: ....

3 blessings to count:

1. ....

2. ....

3. ....

3 ways to bless others:

1. ....

2. ....

3. ....

today is: ....

3 blessings to count:

1. ....

2. ....

3. ....

3 ways to bless others:

1. ....

2. ....

3. ....

today is: ....

3 blessings to count:

1. ....

2. ....

3. ....

3 ways to bless others:

1. ....

2. ....

3. ....

"Worship the Lord your God,
and his blessing will be on your food and water.
I will take away sickness from among you."

— Exodus 23:25

today is: ....

3 blessings to count:

   1. ....

   2. ....

   3. ....

3 ways to bless others:

   1. ....

   2. ....

   3. ....

today is: ....

3 blessings to count:

   1. ....

   2. ....

   3. ....

3 ways to bless others:

   1. ....

   2. ....

   3. ....

today is: ....

3 blessings to count:

   1. ....

   2. ....

   3. ....

3 ways to bless others:

   1. ....

   2. ....

   3. ....

today is: ....

3 blessings to count:

   1. ....

   2. ....

   3. ....

3 ways to bless others:

   1. ....

   2. ....

   3. ....

"But blessed is the one who trusts in the Lord,
whose confidence is in him."

— Jeremiah 17:7

today is: ....

3 blessings to count:

1. ....

2. ....

3. ....

3 ways to bless others:

1. ....

2. ....

3. ....

today is: ....

3 blessings to count:

1. ....

2. ....

3. ....

3 ways to bless others:

1. ....

2. ....

3. ....

today is: ....

3 blessings to count:

1. ....

2. ....

3. ....

3 ways to bless others:

1. ....

2. ....

3. ....

today is: ....

3 blessings to count:

1. ....

2. ....

3. ....

3 ways to bless others:

1. ....

2. ....

3. ....

"Though I walk in the midst of trouble, you preserve my life.
You stretch out your hand against the anger of my foes;
with your right hand you save me."

— Psalm 138:7

today is: ....

3 blessings to count:

1. ....

2. ....

3. ....

3 ways to bless others:

1. ....

2. ....

3. ....

today is: ....

3 blessings to count:

1. ....

2. ....

3. ....

3 ways to bless others:

1. ....

2. ....

3. ....

today is: ....

3 blessings to count:

1. ....

2. ....

3. ....

3 ways to bless others:

1. ....

2. ....

3. ....

today is: ....

3 blessings to count:

1. ....

2. ....

3. ....

3 ways to bless others:

1. ....

2. ....

3. ....

"This is the confidence we have in approaching God;
that if we ask anything according to his will, he hears us."

— 1 John 5:14

today is: ....

3 blessings to count:

1. ....

2. ....

3. ....

3 ways to bless others:

1. ....

2. ....

3. ....

today is: ....

3 blessings to count:

1. ....

2. ....

3. ....

3 ways to bless others:

1. ....

2. ....

3. ....

today is: ....

3 blessings to count:

1. ....

2. ....

3. ....

3 ways to bless others:

1. ....

2. ....

3. ....

today is: ....

3 blessings to count:

1. ....

2. ....

3. ....

3 ways to bless others:

1. ....

2. ....

3. ....

"My God is my rock, in whom I take refuge,
my shield and the horn of my salvation.
He is my stronghold, my refuge and my savior."

— Samuel 22:3

today is: ....

3 blessings to count:

   1. ....

   2. ....

   3. ....

3 ways to bless others:

   1. ....

   2. ....

   3. ....

today is: ....

3 blessings to count:

   1. ....

   2. ....

   3. ....

3 ways to bless others:

   1. ....

   2. ....

   3. ....

today is: ....

3 blessings to count:

   1. ....

   2. ....

   3. ....

3 ways to bless others:

   1. ....

   2. ....

   3. ....

today is: ....

3 blessings to count:

   1. ....

   2. ....

   3. ....

3 ways to bless others:

   1. ....

   2. ....

   3. ....

"Blessed is the nation whose God is the Lord,
the people he chose for his inheritance."
— Psalm 33:12

🌾 today is: ....

3 blessings to count:

  1. ....

  2. ....

  3. ....

3 ways to bless others:

  1. ....

  2. ....

  3. ....

🌸 today is: ....

3 blessings to count:

  1. ....

  2. ....

  3. ....

3 ways to bless others:

  1. ....

  2. ....

  3. ....

🌿 today is: ....

3 blessings to count:

  1. ....

  2. ....

  3. ....

3 ways to bless others:

  1. ....

  2. ....

  3. ....

🌼 today is: ....

3 blessings to count:

  1. ....

  2. ....

  3. ....

3 ways to bless others:

  1. ....

  2. ....

  3. ....

"Listen, my son, accept what I say,
and the years of your life will be many."

— Proverbs 4:19

today is: ....

3 blessings to count:

1. ....
2. ....
3. ....

3 ways to bless others:

1. ....
2. ....
3. ....

today is: ....

3 blessings to count:

1. ....
2. ....
3. ....

3 ways to bless others:

1. ....
2. ....
3. ....

today is: ....

3 blessings to count:

1. ....
2. ....
3. ....

3 ways to bless others:

1. ....
2. ....
3. ....

today is: ....

3 blessings to count:

1. ....
2. ....
3. ....

3 ways to bless others:

1. ....
2. ....
3. ....

"Those who know your name trust in you,
for you, LORD, have **never forsaken those who seek you.**"

— Psalm 9:10

today is: ....

3 blessings to count:

   1. ....

   2. ....

   3. ....

3 ways to bless others:

   1. ....

   2. ....

   3. ....

today is: ....

3 blessings to count:

   1. ....

   2. ....

   3. ....

3 ways to bless others:

   1. ....

   2. ....

   3. ....

today is: ....

3 blessings to count:

   1. ....

   2. ....

   3. ....

3 ways to bless others:

   1. ....

   2. ....

   3. ....

today is: ....

3 blessings to count:

   1. ....

   2. ....

   3. ....

3 ways to bless others:

   1. ....

   2. ....

   3. ....

"When I am afraid,
I put my trust in you."

— Psalm 56:3

today is: ....

3 blessings to count:

  1. ....

  2. ....

  3. ....

3 ways to bless others:

  1. ....

  2. ....

  3. ....

today is: ....

3 blessings to count:

  1. ....

  2. ....

  3. ....

3 ways to bless others:

  1. ....

  2. ....

  3. ....

today is: ....

3 blessings to count:

  1. ....

  2. ....

  3. ....

3 ways to bless others:

  1. ....

  2. ....

  3. ....

today is: ....

3 blessings to count:

  1. ....

  2. ....

  3. ....

3 ways to bless others:

  1. ....

  2. ....

  3. ....

For by grace

you have been saved through faith.
And this is not your own doing;

it is the gift of God,

not a result of works,

so that no one may boast.

— Psalm 9:1

"Mercy, peace and love
be yours in abundance."

— Jude 1:2

today is: ....

3 blessings to count:

1. ....
2. ....
3. ....

3 ways to bless others:

1. ....
2. ....
3. ....

today is: ....

3 blessings to count:

1. ....
2. ....
3. ....

3 ways to bless others:

1. ....
2. ....
3. ....

today is: ....

3 blessings to count:

1. ....
2. ....
3. ....

3 ways to bless others:

1. ....
2. ....
3. ....

today is: ....

3 blessings to count:

1. ....
2. ....
3. ....

3 ways to bless others:

1. ....
2. ....
3. ....

"Those who trust in the Lord are like Mount Zion,
which **cannot be shaken** but **endures forever.**"

— Psalm 125:1

🌿 today is: ....

3 blessings to count:

1. ....

2. ....

3. ....

3 ways to bless others:

1. ....

2. ....

3. ....

🥚 today is: ....

3 blessings to count:

1. ....

2. ....

3. ....

3 ways to bless others:

1. ....

2. ....

3. ....

🌹 today is: ....

3 blessings to count:

1. ....

2. ....

3. ....

3 ways to bless others:

1. ....

2. ....

3. ....

🌷 today is: ....

3 blessings to count:

1. ....

2. ....

3. ....

3 ways to bless others:

1. ....

2. ....

3. ....

"But those who hope in the Lord will renew their strength.
They will **soar on wings like eagles**, they will **run and not grow weary,**
they will **walk and not be faint.**"

— Isaiah 40:31

---

today is: ....

3 blessings to count:

1. ....

2. ....

3. ....

3 ways to bless others:

1. ....

2. ....

3. ....

---

today is: ....

3 blessings to count:

1. ....

2. ....

3. ....

3 ways to bless others:

1. ....

2. ....

3. ....

---

today is: ....

3 blessings to count:

1. ....

2. ....

3. ....

3 ways to bless others:

1. ....

2. ....

3. ....

---

today is: ....

3 blessings to count:

1. ....

2. ....

3. ....

3 ways to bless others:

1. ....

2. ....

3. ....

"Give thanks to the Lord, for he is good.
His love endures forever."
— Psalm 136:1

---

today is: ....

3 blessings to count:

1. ....

2. ....

3. ....

3 ways to bless others:

1. ....

2. ....

3. ....

---

today is: ....

3 blessings to count:

1. ....

2. ....

3. ....

3 ways to bless others:

1. ....

2. ....

3. ....

---

today is: ....

3 blessings to count:

1. ....

2. ....

3. ....

3 ways to bless others:

1. ....

2. ....

3. ....

---

today is: ....

3 blessings to count:

1. ....

2. ....

3. ....

3 ways to bless others:

1. ....

2. ....

3. ....

"So whether you eat or drink or whatever you do,
do it all for the glory of God."

— Corinthians 10:30

today is: ....

3 blessings to count:

1. ....
2. ....
3. ....

3 ways to bless others:

1. ....
2. ....
3. ....

today is: ....

3 blessings to count:

1. ....
2. ....
3. ....

3 ways to bless others:

1. ....
2. ....
3. ....

today is: ....

3 blessings to count:

1. ....
2. ....
3. ....

3 ways to bless others:

1. ....
2. ....
3. ....

today is: ....

3 blessings to count:

1. ....
2. ....
3. ....

3 ways to bless others:

1. ....
2. ....
3. ....

"So do not fear, for I am with you;
do not be dismayed, for I am your God. I will strengthen you and help you;
for I will uphold you with my righteous right hand."

— Isaiah 41:10

today is: ....

3 blessings to count:

1. ....

2. ....

3. ....

3 ways to bless others:

1. ....

2. ....

3. ....

today is: ....

3 blessings to count:

1. ....

2. ....

3. ....

3 ways to bless others:

1. ....

2. ....

3. ....

today is: ....

3 blessings to count:

1. ....

2. ....

3. ....

3 ways to bless others:

1. ....

2. ....

3. ....

today is: ....

3 blessings to count:

1. ....

2. ....

3. ....

3 ways to bless others:

1. ....

2. ....

3. ....

"Let your roots grow down into him, and let your lives be built on him.
Then your faith will grow strong in the truth you were taught,
and you will overflow with thankfulness."

— Colossians 2:7

today is: ....

3 blessings to count:

1. ....

2. ....

3. ....

3 ways to bless others:

1. ....

2. ....

3. ....

today is: ....

3 blessings to count:

1. ....

2. ....

3. ....

3 ways to bless others:

1. ....

2. ....

3. ....

today is: ....

3 blessings to count:

1. ....

2. ....

3. ....

3 ways to bless others:

1. ....

2. ....

3. ....

today is: ....

3 blessings to count:

1. ....

2. ....

3. ....

3 ways to bless others:

1. ....

2. ....

3. ....

"And hope does not put us to shame,
because God's love has been poured out into our hearts
through the Holy Spirit, who has been given to us."

— Romans 5:5

◯ today is: ....

3 blessings to count:

1. ....

2. ....

3. ....

3 ways to bless others:

1. ....

2. ....

3. ....

🌿 today is: ....

3 blessings to count:

1. ....

2. ....

3. ....

3 ways to bless others:

1. ....

2. ....

3. ....

🖊 today is: ....

3 blessings to count:

1. ....

2. ....

3. ....

3 ways to bless others:

1. ....

2. ....

3. ....

⚒ today is: ....

3 blessings to count:

1. ....

2. ....

3. ....

3 ways to bless others:

1. ....

2. ....

3. ....

When I am afraid,
I put my
trust
in you.

— Psalm 56:3

"Because you know that the testing of your faith produces perseverance.
Let perseverance finish its work
so that you may be mature and complete, not lacking anything."

— James 1:3-4

today is: ....

3 blessings to count:

   1. ....

   2. ....

   3. ....

3 ways to bless others:

   1. ....

   2. ....

   3. ....

today is: ....

3 blessings to count:

   1. ....

   2. ....

   3. ....

3 ways to bless others:

   1. ....

   2. ....

   3. ....

today is: ....

3 blessings to count:

   1. ....

   2. ....

   3. ....

3 ways to bless others:

   1. ....

   2. ....

   3. ....

today is: ....

3 blessings to count:

   1. ....

   2. ....

   3. ....

3 ways to bless others:

   1. ....

   2. ....

   3. ....

"But thanks be to God!
He gives us the victory through our Lord Jesus Christ."

— 1 Corinthians 15:57

today is: ....

3 blessings to count:

1. ....

2. ....

3. ....

3 ways to bless others:

1. ....

2. ....

3. ....

today is: ....

3 blessings to count:

1. ....

2. ....

3. ....

3 ways to bless others:

1. ....

2. ....

3. ....

today is: ....

3 blessings to count:

1. ....

2. ....

3. ....

3 ways to bless others:

1. ....

2. ....

3. ....

today is: ....

3 blessings to count:

1. ....

2. ....

3. ....

3 ways to bless others:

1. ....

2. ....

3. ....

"And giving joyful thanks to the Father,
who has qualified you to share in the inheritance of his holy people
in the kingdom of light."
— Colossians 1:12

today is: ....

3 blessings to count:

   1. ....

   2. ....

   3. ....

3 ways to bless others:

   1. ....

   2. ....

   3. ....

today is: ....

3 blessings to count:

   1. ....

   2. ....

   3. ....

3 ways to bless others:

   1. ....

   2. ....

   3. ....

today is: ....

3 blessings to count:

   1. ....

   2. ....

   3. ....

3 ways to bless others:

   1. ....

   2. ....

   3. ....

today is: ....

3 blessings to count:

   1. ....

   2. ....

   3. ....

3 ways to bless others:

   1. ....

   2. ....

   3. ....

"Saying: 'We give thanks to you, Lord God Almighty,
the One who is and who was,
because you have taken your great power and have begun to reign.'"

— Ephesians 5:20

today is: ....

3 blessings to count:

1. ....

2. ....

3. ....

3 ways to bless others:

1. ....

2. ....

3. ....

today is: ....

3 blessings to count:

1. ....

2. ....

3. ....

3 ways to bless others:

1. ....

2. ....

3. ....

today is: ....

3 blessings to count:

1. ....

2. ....

3. ....

3 ways to bless others:

1. ....

2. ....

3. ....

today is: ....

3 blessings to count:

1. ....

2. ....

3. ....

3 ways to bless others:

1. ....

2. ....

3. ....

"Let them sacrifice thank offerings and
tell of his works with songs of joy."
— Psalm 107:22

today is: ....

3 blessings to count:
   1. ....
   2. ....
   3. ....

3 ways to bless others:
   1. ....
   2. ....
   3. ....

today is: ....

3 blessings to count:
   1. ....
   2. ....
   3. ....

3 ways to bless others:
   1. ....
   2. ....
   3. ....

today is: ....

3 blessings to count:
   1. ....
   2. ....
   3. ....

3 ways to bless others:
   1. ....
   2. ....
   3. ....

today is: ....

3 blessings to count:
   1. ....
   2. ....
   3. ....

3 ways to bless others:
   1. ....
   2. ....
   3. ....

"I will **praise** God's name in song
and **glorify** him with thanksgiving."
— Psalm 69:30

---

today is: ....

3 blessings to count:

1. ....

2. ....

3. ....

3 ways to bless others:

1. ....

2. ....

3. ....

---

today is: ....

3 blessings to count:

1. ....

2. ....

3. ....

3 ways to bless others:

1. ....

2. ....

3. ....

---

today is: ....

3 blessings to count:

1. ....

2. ....

3. ....

3 ways to bless others:

1. ....

2. ....

3. ....

---

today is: ....

3 blessings to count:

1. ....

2. ....

3. ....

3 ways to bless others:

1. ....

2. ....

3. ....

"Whenever the living creatures give glory, honor and thanks to him who sits on the throne and who lives for ever and ever."

— Revelation 4:9

today is: ....

3 blessings to count:

   1. ....

   2. ....

   3. ....

3 ways to bless others:

   1. ....

   2. ....

   3. ....

today is: ....

3 blessings to count:

   1. ....

   2. ....

   3. ....

3 ways to bless others:

   1. ....

   2. ....

   3. ....

today is: ....

3 blessings to count:

   1. ....

   2. ....

   3. ....

3 ways to bless others:

   1. ....

   2. ....

   3. ....

today is: ....

3 blessings to count:

   1. ....

   2. ....

   3. ....

3 ways to bless others:

   1. ....

   2. ....

   3. ....

A good man *brings* good things
out of the good *stored* up in his heart...
for **the mouth** speaks
what **the heart**
is **full** of.

— Luke 6:45

"Through Jesus, therefore, let us continually offer to God a sacrifice of praise—
the fruit of lips that openly profess his name."

— Hebrews 13:15

today is: ....

3 blessings to count:

1. ....
2. ....
3. ....

3 ways to bless others:

1. ....
2. ....
3. ....

today is: ....

3 blessings to count:

1. ....
2. ....
3. ....

3 ways to bless others:

1. ....
2. ....
3. ....

today is: ....

3 blessings to count:

1. ....
2. ....
3. ....

3 ways to bless others:

1. ....
2. ....
3. ....

today is: ....

3 blessings to count:

1. ....
2. ....
3. ....

3 ways to bless others:

1. ....
2. ....
3. ....

"For what you have done I will always praise you
in the presence of your faithful people.
And I will hope in your name, for your name is good."

— Psalm 52:9

today is: ....

3 blessings to count:

1. ....

2. ....

3. ....

3 ways to bless others:

1. ....

2. ....

3. ....

today is: ....

3 blessings to count:

1. ....

2. ....

3. ....

3 ways to bless others:

1. ....

2. ....

3. ....

today is: ....

3 blessings to count:

1. ....

2. ....

3. ....

3 ways to bless others:

1. ....

2. ....

3. ....

today is: ....

3 blessings to count:

1. ....

2. ....

3. ....

3 ways to bless others:

1. ....

2. ....

3. ....

"Sing to the LORD with grateful praise;
make music to our God on the harp."

— Psalm 147:7

---

today is: ....

3 blessings to count:

1. ....

2. ....

3. ....

3 ways to bless others:

1. ....

2. ....

3. ....

---

today is: ....

3 blessings to count:

1. ....

2. ....

3. ....

3 ways to bless others:

1. ....

2. ....

3. ....

---

today is: ....

3 blessings to count:

1. ....

2. ....

3. ....

3 ways to bless others:

1. ....

2. ....

3. ....

---

today is: ....

3 blessings to count:

1. ....

2. ....

3. ....

3 ways to bless others:

1. ....

2. ....

3. ....

"For by grace you have been saved through faith.
And this is not your own doing; it is the gift of God,
not a result of works, so that no one may boast."

— Psalm 9:1

---

today is: ....

3 blessings to count:

1. ....

2. ....

3. ....

3 ways to bless others:

1. ....

2. ....

3. ....

---

today is: ....

3 blessings to count:

1. ....

2. ....

3. ....

3 ways to bless others:

1. ....

2. ....

3. ....

---

today is: ....

3 blessings to count:

1. ....

2. ....

3. ....

3 ways to bless others:

1. ....

2. ....

3. ....

---

today is: ....

3 blessings to count:

1. ....

2. ....

3. ....

3 ways to bless others:

1. ....

2. ....

3. ....

"May **mercy** and **peace** and love
be multiplied to you."

— Jude 1:2

today is: ....

3 blessings to count:

  1. ....

  2. ....

  3. ....

3 ways to bless others:

  1. ....

  2. ....

  3. ....

today is: ....

3 blessings to count:

  1. ....

  2. ....

  3. ....

3 ways to bless others:

  1. ....

  2. ....

  3. ....

today is: ....

3 blessings to count:

  1. ....

  2. ....

  3. ....

3 ways to bless others:

  1. ....

  2. ....

  3. ....

today is: ....

3 blessings to count:

  1. ....

  2. ....

  3. ....

3 ways to bless others:

  1. ....

  2. ....

  3. ....

"A good man brings good things out of the good stored up in his heart...
for the mouth speaks what the heart is full of."
— Luke 6:45

🌿 today is: ....

3 blessings to count:

1. ....

2. ....

3. ....

3 ways to bless others:

1. ....

2. ....

3. ....

◯ today is: ....

3 blessings to count:

1. ....

2. ....

3. ....

3 ways to bless others:

1. ....

2. ....

3. ....

✏️ today is: ....

3 blessings to count:

1. ....

2. ....

3. ....

3 ways to bless others:

1. ....

2. ....

3. ....

🌱 today is: ....

3 blessings to count:

1. ....

2. ....

3. ....

3 ways to bless others:

1. ....

2. ....

3. ....

"You made men ride over our heads;
We went through fire and through water,
Yet You brought us out into a place of abundance."
— Colossians 4:2

---

today is: ....

3 blessings to count:

1. ....

2. ....

3. ....

3 ways to bless others:

1. ....

2. ....

3. ....

---

today is: ....

3 blessings to count:

1. ....

2. ....

3. ....

3 ways to bless others:

1. ....

2. ....

3. ....

---

today is: ....

3 blessings to count:

1. ....

2. ....

3. ....

3 ways to bless others:

1. ....

2. ....

3. ....

---

today is: ....

3 blessings to count:

1. ....

2. ....

3. ....

3 ways to bless others:

1. ....

2. ....

3. ....

"Let us come before him with thanksgiving and extol him with music and song. For the LORD is the great God, the great King above all gods."

— Psalm 95:2-3

🌸 today is: ....

3 blessings to count:

1. ....
2. ....
3. ....

3 ways to bless others:

1. ....
2. ....
3. ....

🥚 today is: ....

3 blessings to count:

1. ....
2. ....
3. ....

3 ways to bless others:

1. ....
2. ....
3. ....

🌿 today is: ....

3 blessings to count:

1. ....
2. ....
3. ....

3 ways to bless others:

1. ....
2. ....
3. ....

🌱 today is: ....

3 blessings to count:

1. ....
2. ....
3. ....

3 ways to bless others:

1. ....
2. ....
3. ....

"Rejoice evermore. Pray without ceasing.
In every thing give thanks:
for this is the will of God in Christ Jesus concerning you."

— 1 Thessalonians 5:16-18

today is: ....

3 blessings to count:

1. ....

2. ....

3. ....

3 ways to bless others:

1. ....

2. ....

3. ....

today is: ....

3 blessings to count:

1. ....

2. ....

3. ....

3 ways to bless others:

1. ....

2. ....

3. ....

today is: ....

3 blessings to count:

1. ....

2. ....

3. ....

3 ways to bless others:

1. ....

2. ....

3. ....

today is: ....

3 blessings to count:

1. ....

2. ....

3. ....

3 ways to bless others:

1. ....

2. ....

3. ....

"And God is able to bless you abundantly,
so that in all things at all times, having all that you need,
you will abound in every good work."

— 2 Corinthians 9:8

today is: ....

3 blessings to count:

1. ....

2. ....

3. ....

3 ways to bless others:

1. ....

2. ....

3. ....

today is: ....

3 blessings to count:

1. ....

2. ....

3. ....

3 ways to bless others:

1. ....

2. ....

3. ....

today is: ....

3 blessings to count:

1. ....

2. ....

3. ....

3 ways to bless others:

1. ....

2. ....

3. ....

today is: ....

3 blessings to count:

1. ....

2. ....

3. ....

3 ways to bless others:

1. ....

2. ....

3. ....

"It is of the Lord's mercies that we are not consumed,
because his compassions fail not.
They are new every morning: great is thy faithfulness."
— Lamentations 3:22-23

today is:.....................

3 blessings to count:

1. ....

2. ....

3. ....

3 ways to bless others:

1. ....

2. ....

3. ....

today is:.....................

3 blessings to count:

1. ....

2. ....

3. ....

3 ways to bless others:

1. ....

2. ....

3. ....

today is:.....................

3 blessings to count:

1. ....

2. ....

3. ....

3 ways to bless others:

1. ....

2. ....

3. ....

today is:.....................

3 blessings to count:

1. ....

2. ....

3. ....

3 ways to bless others:

1. ....

2. ....

3. ....

"Every good gift and every perfect gift is from above,

and cometh down from the Father of lights,
with whom is no variableness, neither shadow of turning."

— James 1:17

today is: ....

3 blessings to count:

  1. ....
  2. ....
  3. ....

3 ways to bless others:

  1. ....
  2. ....
  3. ....

today is: ....

3 blessings to count:

  1. ....
  2. ....
  3. ....

3 ways to bless others:

  1. ....
  2. ....
  3. ....

today is: ....

3 blessings to count:

  1. ....
  2. ....
  3. ....

3 ways to bless others:

  1. ....
  2. ....
  3. ....

today is: ....

3 blessings to count:

  1. ....
  2. ....
  3. ....

3 ways to bless others:

  1. ....
  2. ....
  3. ....

"O give thanks unto the Lord, for he is good:
for his mercy endureth forever."

— Psalm 107:1

today is: ....

3 blessings to count:

1. ....
2. ....
3. ....

3 ways to bless others:

1. ....
2. ....
3. ....

today is: ....

3 blessings to count:

1. ....
2. ....
3. ....

3 ways to bless others:

1. ....
2. ....
3. ....

today is: ....

3 blessings to count:

1. ....
2. ....
3. ....

3 ways to bless others:

1. ....
2. ....
3. ....

today is: ....

3 blessings to count:

1. ....
2. ....
3. ....

3 ways to bless others:

1. ....
2. ....
3. ....

"All this is for your benefit,
so that the grace that is reaching more and more people may cause
thanksgiving to overflow to the glory of God."
— 2 Corinthians 4:15

today is: ....

3 blessings to count:

   1. ....
   2. ....
   3. ....

3 ways to bless others:

   1. ....
   2. ....
   3. ....

today is: ....

3 blessings to count:

   1. ....
   2. ....
   3. ....

3 ways to bless others:

   1. ....
   2. ....
   3. ....

today is: ....

3 blessings to count:

   1. ....
   2. ....
   3. ....

3 ways to bless others:

   1. ....
   2. ....
   3. ....

today is: ....

3 blessings to count:

   1. ....
   2. ....
   3. ....

3 ways to bless others:

   1. ....
   2. ....
   3. ....

"You crown the year with your bounty,
and your carts overflow with abundance."

— Psalm 65:11

🪡 **today is:** ....

3 blessings to count:

   1. ....

   2. ....

   3. ....

3 ways to bless others:

   1. ....

   2. ....

   3. ....

🌿 **today is:** ....

3 blessings to count:

   1. ....

   2. ....

   3. ....

3 ways to bless others:

   1. ....

   2. ....

   3. ....

🌾 **today is:** ....

3 blessings to count:

   1. ....

   2. ....

   3. ....

3 ways to bless others:

   1. ....

   2. ....

   3. ....

🌱 **today is:** ....

3 blessings to count:

   1. ....

   2. ....

   3. ....

3 ways to bless others:

   1. ....

   2. ....

   3. ....

"I will sacrifice a freewill offering to you;
I will praise your name, Lord, for **it is good**."

— Psalm 54:6

today is: ....

3 blessings to count:

1. ....

2. ....

3. ....

3 ways to bless others:

1. ....

2. ....

3. ....

today is: ....

3 blessings to count:

1. ....

2. ....

3. ....

3 ways to bless others:

1. ....

2. ....

3. ....

today is: ....

3 blessings to count:

1. ....

2. ....

3. ....

3 ways to bless others:

1. ....

2. ....

3. ....

today is: ....

3 blessings to count:

1. ....

2. ....

3. ....

3 ways to bless others:

1. ....

2. ....

3. ....

"The one who **offers thanksgiving as his sacrifice**
glorifies me; to one who orders his way rightly
I will show the salvation of God!"

— Psalm 50:23

today is: ....

3 blessings to count:

1. ....

2. ....

3. ....

3 ways to bless others:

1. ....

2. ....

3. ....

today is: ....

3 blessings to count:

1. ....

2. ....

3. ....

3 ways to bless others:

1. ....

2. ....

3. ....

today is: ....

3 blessings to count:

1. ....

2. ....

3. ....

3 ways to bless others:

1. ....

2. ....

3. ....

today is: ....

3 blessings to count:

1. ....

2. ....

3. ....

3 ways to bless others:

1. ....

2. ....

3. ....

"Let them give thanks to the Lord

for his unfailing love and his wonderful deeds for mankind."

— Psalm 107:21

⊸≫⊱⊰≪⊷ **today is:** ....

3 blessings to count:

1. ....

2. ....

3. ....

3 ways to bless others:

1. ....

2. ....

3. ....

---

today is: ....

3 blessings to count:

1. ....

2. ....

3. ....

3 ways to bless others:

1. ....

2. ....

3. ....

---

today is: ....

3 blessings to count:

1. ....

2. ....

3. ....

3 ways to bless others:

1. ....

2. ....

3. ....

---

today is: ....

3 blessings to count:

1. ....

2. ....

3. ....

3 ways to bless others:

1. ....

2. ....

3. ....

I'm grateful to you for buying & using this journal!

If you got some joy out of it, would you consider sharing it with others by leaving an Amazon review? It's the best way to help other people find this journal and bring more gratitude to their lives!

You can use this link to leave a review on Amazon:

http://bit.ly/blessingsjournal

or go to the page where you bought it and click "Leave a review."

THANK YOU!
Mia

Made in the USA
Middletown, DE
11 March 2024

51297424R00062